DISCOVER AND DO!

MATERIALS

Written by Jane Lacey

Enslow PUBLISHING

Published in 2023 by Enslow Publishing, LLC
29 East 21st Street, New York, NY 10010

Editor: Katie Dicker
Series Designer: Rocket Design (East Anglia) Ltd

Manufactured in the United States of America

CPSIA compliance information: Batch #CSENS23: For further information contact Enslow Publishing LLC, New York, New York at 1-800-398-2504.

Please visit our website, www.enslowpublishing.com. For a free color catalog of all our high-quality books, call toll free 1-800-398-2504 or fax 1-877-980-4454.

Cataloging-in-Publication Data
Names: Lacey, Jane.

Title: Materials / Jane Lacey.

Description: New York : Enslow Publishing, 2023. | Series: Discover and do! | Includes glossary and index.

Identifiers: ISBN 9781978530706 (pbk.) | ISBN 9781978530720 (library bound) | ISBN 9781978530713 (6pack) | ISBN 9781978530737 (ebook)

Subjects: LCSH: Materials--Juvenile literature.

Classification: LCC TA403.2 L334 2023 | DDC 620--dc23

Picture credits:

t=top b=bottom m=middle l=left r=right

Shutterstock: Oceloti cover/title page l, Marko Petrusevski cover/title page r, Akane1988 5tl and 18bl, vertolena 5tr and 10tr, Tatyana Prokofieva 5br, 7tr, 28 and 31m, Roi and Roi 6tr, ClassicVector 6ml, Oleksandr Derevianko 6–7b, iDraw 8tr and 31b, charless 9tr, Stuart Miles 9bl, vetoslav Iliev 9br, Unitone Vector 10br, Kjolak 10bm, Haver 10bl, Mego studio 12tr, Forgem 12b, 14tr, Lemberg Vector studio 14b, Jakinnboaz 15tr, Kateyka 16b, Macrovector 16bm, Breck P. Kent 17tr, Tubeliaieva 18tr, peart.ru 18br, asilyeva Larisa 18bl, GOLFX 19bl, Stefan Malloch 20tr and 32, kolopach 21tl and 29tr, ffolas 21bl, Iconic Bestiary 22b, solar22 23tr, nito 24tr, Yauhen Paleski 26b and 31t, Grimgram 27, Bonezboyz 27, puaypuay 27, WindAwake 27, sabri deniz kizil 27; Getty: alazur 4 and 8b, akkachai thothubthai 16tr and 30b, LeoPride 18bm, blueringmedia 19tr and 30t, UnitoneVector 20b, seamartini 22tr, Feodora Chiosea 24b, IconicBestiary 26mr and 29br.

All design elements from Shutterstock.

Craft models from a previous series by Q2AMedia.

DISCOVER AND DO!

MATERIALS

Written by Jane Lacey

Enslow PUBLISHING

Contents

Words that appear in **bold** can be found in the glossary on pages 28–29.

WHAT ARE MATERIALS?

Things that have been made, such as books and clothes and cars, all come from materials. Paper is the material used to make books, cotton is what is used to make shirts, and cars are made of metal.

Books are made from paper that comes from trees.

Natural materials

Some materials are natural. They come from animals or plants or they are found in the ground. Wool comes from the soft coats of sheep, wood from the trunks of trees, and marble is a kind of rock.

When a sheep is sheared, or cut off, the soft wool is spun to make wool yarn.

Made materials

Some materials are made from other materials. Glass is a **mixture** of sand and **limestone** that has been heated. Plastic is made from oil. Paper is made from small chips of wood and water.

These brightly colored toys are made from strong, light plastic.

Right for the job

Materials are chosen for the kind of job they have to do. Soft, warm wool is used to make winter coats and sweaters. Tough metal is used to make strong, long-lasting bridges.

This metal bridge is strong enough to carry traffic. It also bends without breaking in high winds.

WHAT IS A SOLID?

Materials come in three different forms: solid, liquid, or gas. A solid is able to hold a shape. Some solid materials, such as wood or clay, can be cut or molded to change their shape.

Weight and size

Solid objects can be light or heavy for their size, depending on the material they are made from. **Polystyrene foam**, for example, is full of air pockets. This makes it light to carry.

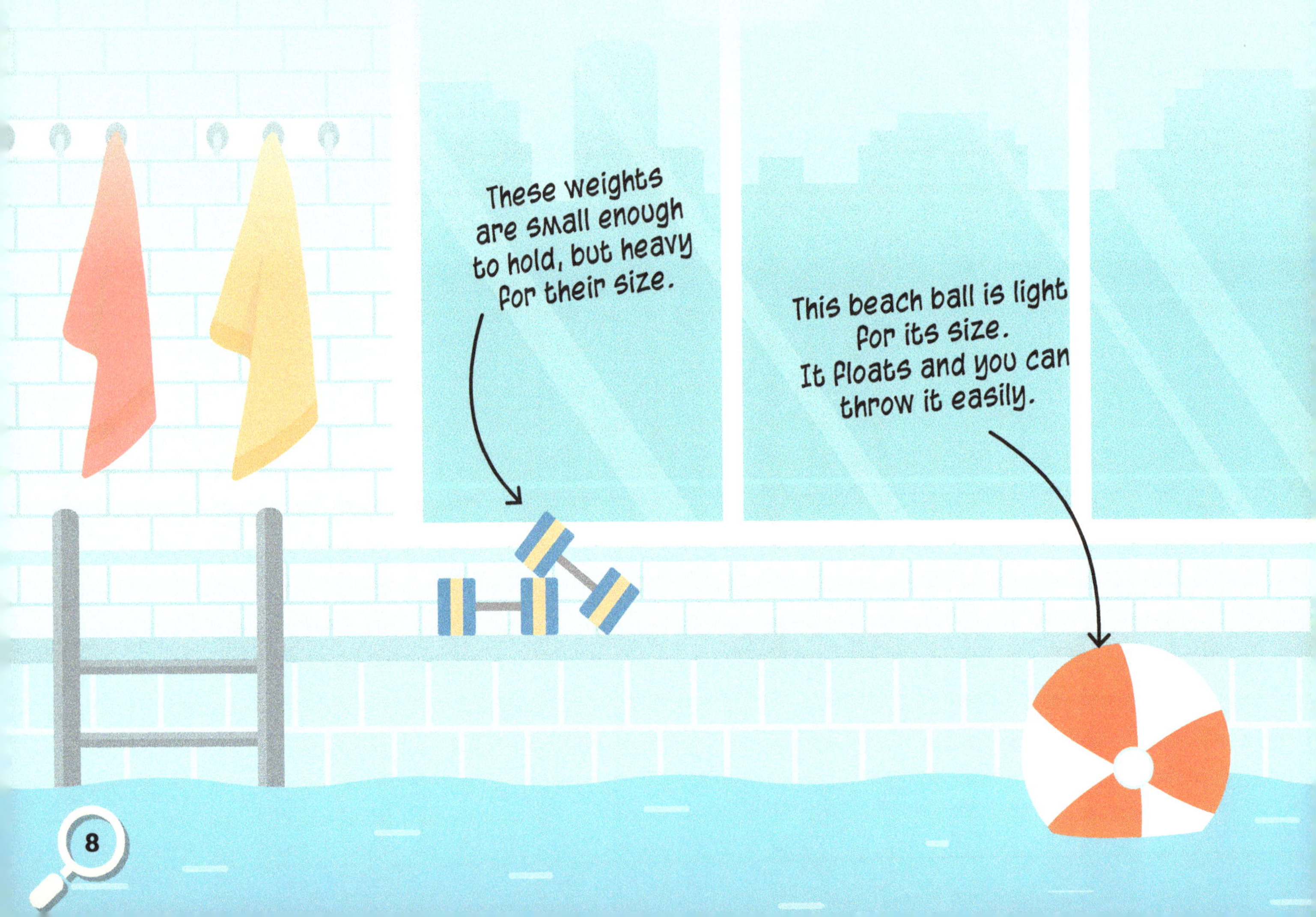

Properties of materials

Solid materials have different qualities or **properties**. For example, they can be hard or soft, **waterproof** or **absorbent**, heavy or light, shiny or dull. These properties make them useful for a particular purpose.

A waterproof shower cap keeps your hair dry, while a soft towel absorbs the water.

ACTIVITY

TEST THE PROPERTIES OF SOLID MATERIALS

You will need:

- **sponge**
- **coin**
- **sheet of plastic**
- **lump of clay**
- **bowl of water**

1. Press and squeeze the sponge, coin, plastic, and clay to find out whether the materials are soft or hard.
2. Put each material in the water to find out which materials float or sink, and which are waterproof or absorbent.
3. Make a chart like the one shown below to record your findings.

Materials float when they are light for their size. Materials that are heavy for their size are not supported by the water, and so they sink.

	Soft	Hard	Waterproof	Absorbent	Float	Sink
Sponge	✓			✓	✓	
Coin						

WHAT IS A LIQUID?

Water, honey, and oil are different kinds of liquid. Liquids flow and pour. Water flows out of a tap when you turn it on. River water pours over a cliff to make a waterfall.

When you pour milk into a glass, the liquid takes the shape of the glass.

No shape of its own

A liquid doesn't have a shape of its own. It takes the shape of whatever container it is in. If you spill your juice, it spreads out and makes a puddle!

Thick and thin

Some liquids are thicker than others and they flow differently. Thin liquids, such as water or milk, flow quickly and splash when you pour them. Thick liquids, such as honey and oil, pour slowly.

Cake icing is runny but gets thicker when it cools down.

A hot chocolate drink pours quickly, while melted chocolate is thicker and takes more time.

ACTIVITY

THE GREAT POURING RACE

You will need:
- **3 clear plastic cups**
- **honey**
- **oil**
- **dish soap**
- **ruler**
- **tape**
- **cutting board**
- **pile of books**
- **large bowl**

1. Fill the cups up about a third of the way, one with honey, one with oil, and one with dish soap.

2. Tape the cups firmly to a ruler (as shown above).

3. Lean the chopping board against some books and the bowl to make a slope.

4. Tip the ruler gently so the liquids start to pour out of the cups onto the top of the slope. Which liquid wins the pouring race?

You will find that the liquids move at different speeds down the slope. Thin liquids move quickly. Thick liquids take longer to reach the bottom of the slope.

WHAT IS A GAS?

Gases are often difficult to see, smell, or feel, but they are just as real as solids and liquids. The air around us is a mixture of gases. We breathe air in and out of our lungs.

Air from your lungs squeezes into a balloon when you blow it up.

Moving and flowing

Gases have no shape of their own. As they flow and move around, they spread to fill whatever container they are in. Gases can also be compressed (squeezed) to take up less space.

Hot air

When air heats up, it **expands,** or spreads out, and becomes lighter than cold air. Lighter hot air rises above heavier cold air.

Hot air makes this balloon rise. When the air cools, the balloon will sink back down to the ground.

ACTIVITY

CREATE A GAS AND MAKE A VOLCANO ERUPT

You will need:

- small plastic bottle
- large tray
- self-hardening clay
- waterproof paints and brush
- 4 tablespoons (50 g) baking soda
- jug with a mixture of 1/2 cup (125 ml) warm water, 1/4 cup (60 ml) dish soap, and a few drops of red food coloring
- 2 tablespoons (30 ml) of vinegar

1. Stand the empty bottle on the tray. Build a volcano shape around it with the clay, leaving the top of the bottle open. When the clay is dry, paint your volcano.

2. Put the baking soda in the bottle and pour in the liquid mixture.

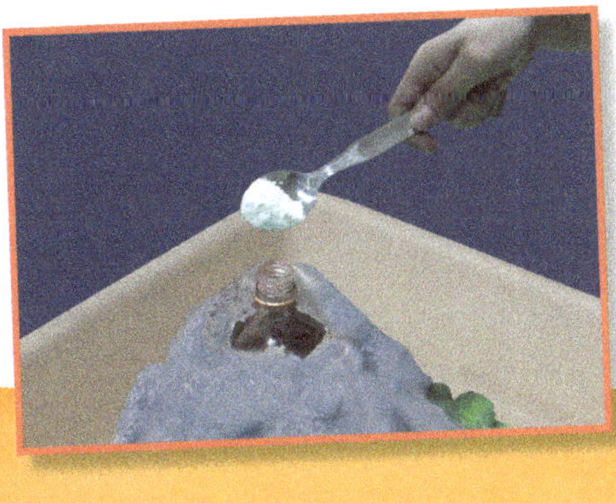

3. Now add the vinegar and stand back! Watch your volcano erupt.

When the vinegar and the baking soda mix, they create bubbles of a gas called **carbon dioxide**, making it fizz up out of the volcano.

WATER

Water can be a solid, a liquid, or a gas. Ice is solid water. Liquid water is found in rivers, lakes, and oceans. An invisible gas called **water vapor** is in the air all around us.

Freezing point

Liquid water **freezes** into solid ice at 32°F (0°C). It stays frozen below that temperature, but will **melt** when the temperature rises above 32°F. An ice cube from the freezer, for example, quickly melts in your drink on a hot day.

Evaporation

When water is warmed by the sun, it **evaporates** and turns into water vapor. Water vapor rises and cools into water droplets that form clouds. Water falls back to Earth as rain, sleet, or snow.

The movement of water as it warms and cools is called the water cycle.

ACTIVITY

MAKE A WATERY PRINT

You will need:

- **ice-cube tray**
- **water**
- **food coloring**
- **absorbent paper (or a white cloth)**
- **large tray**

1. Fill an ice-cube tray with water.

2. Add a few drops of food coloring to some of the cubes and put the tray into a freezer.

3. When the cubes are frozen, put them on the paper on a large tray in the sunshine. Arrange them in a pretty shape or pattern.

As the ice cubes melt, the water will evaporate and leave a colored watery pattern on the paper or cloth.

MIXTURES AND SOLUTIONS

All kinds of things are mixtures. Sand is a mixture of broken rock and sea shells. Soil is a mixture of broken rock, dead animals, and plants. Even cereal can be a mixture of grains, nuts, and fruit.

If you look closely at sand, you can see tiny pieces of shell among the grains.

Solutions

Some things **dissolve** in water. This means they mix completely and make a **solution**. Sugar dissolves in a cup of hot tea. Salt dissolves in hot soup. You can't see the sugar or salt, but you can taste them.

Sea water is a solution of water and **minerals**. It tastes salty and is not good to drink!

Stalagmites and stalactites

Stalagmites and **stalactites** can be found in caves. They form when water drips off the cave roof onto the floor. Minerals that were dissolved in the water are left behind when the water evaporates. They create columns that have strange shapes!

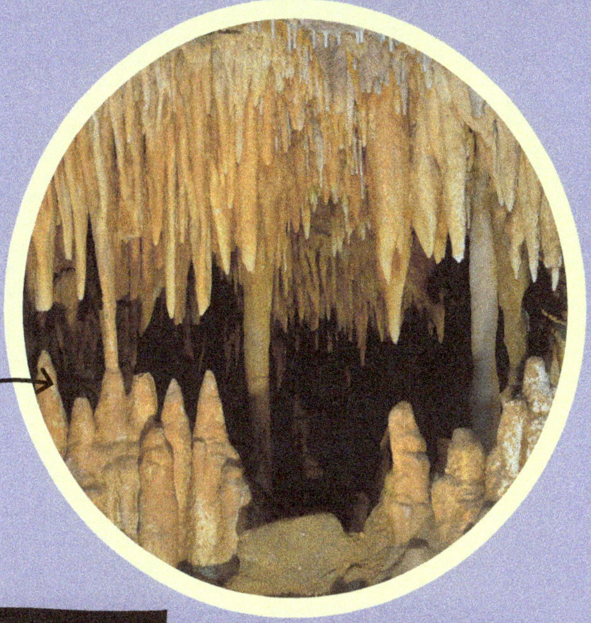

Stalagmites (bottom) and stalactites (top) take thousands of years to form.

ACTIVITY

MAKE A STALACTITE

You will need:
- **2 small jars**
- **warm water**
- **baking soda**
- **spoon**
- **2 pieces of yarn about 1 foot (30 cm) long**
- **bowl or plate**

1. Fill the jars with warm water. Gradually add and stir in as much soda as will dissolve to make a solution in each jar.

2. Place the saucer between the jars in a warm place (a sunny windowsill or a shelf above a heating vent). Twist the yarn together and hang one end in each jar.

3. Leave it alone for a few days. Watch crystals of soda form on the yarn, drip onto the saucer, and form a stalactite.

HEAT

Heat changes materials. When metal becomes hot it expands. When paper and wood become very hot, they catch fire. Hot water boils and turns into water vapor.

Cooking

Cooking changes some foods in such a way that they can't be changed back again. When bread is toasted, it becomes harder and turns brown. Crisp vegetables become soft. The white of an egg changes color and becomes firm.

Baking a cake

When we make a cake we often add baking powder to the cake mixture. This produces tiny bubbles of the gas carbon dioxide. In the oven, heat expands the bubbles, and makes the cake mixture rise.

ACTIVITY

BAKE SOME SPONGE CAKES

Ask an adult to help you with this activity.

You will need:
- **large muffin tin**
- **2 mixing bowls**
- **electric beaters**
- **spoon**
- **flour**
- **sugar**
- **butter**
- **baking powder**
- **eggs**
- **oven heated to 350°**

Mixture A • 1/4 cup flour
• 1 egg • 1/4 cup butter
• 1/4 cup sugar

Mixture B • 1/4 cup flour
• 1 teaspoon of baking powder
• 1 egg • 1/4 cup butter
• 1/4 cup sugar

1. Lightly grease the muffin tin.

2. Create mixture A and mixture B (see above right) in two separate mixing bowls. Ask an adult to help you mix the ingredients together.

3. Fill half the muffin tin with mixture A, the other half with mixture B, and bake in the center of the oven for 15 to 20 minutes.

The mixture A cakes will look like flat cookies while the mixture B cakes will have risen. The baking powder helps the cakes to rise.

MELT AND MOLD

Some solid materials, such as glass and plastic, melt and become liquid when they are heated. They become solid again when they cool down. In the meantime, these materials can be melted and molded into new shapes.

Heated glass can be molded into decorative shapes.

Molding shapes

A mold is a container that gives the **molten** glass or plastic its shape. Plastic toys are made using molds. When molten plastic is poured into a mold of a toy spaceship, for example, it hardens into a spaceship shape when it cools.

Food

Butter, chocolate, and cheese all melt when they are hot. A chocolate bar becomes soft and sticky on a warm day. Butter is easier to spread when it is warm than when it is first taken out from a cold fridge.

When a pizza comes out of a hot oven, the cheese has melted.

ACTIVITY

MAKE CHOCOLATE SHAPES

Ask an adult to help you with this activity.

You will need:

- **bar of chocolate**
- **heatproof bowl**
- **pan of water**
- **baking sheet**
- **cookie cutters**
- **margarine or butter**
- **sprinkles**

1. Break the chocolate bar into pieces. Ask an adult to help you melt the chocolate in a bowl over a pan of simmering water.

2. Lightly grease a baking sheet and the inside of some cookie cutters with the margarine or butter.

3. Place the shapes on the tray and carefully pour in the melted chocolate.

4. Decorate and leave to cool.

Share the chocolate shapes with your friends!

SQUEEZE AND STRETCH

You can squeeze and stretch some solid materials to change their shape. Clay is good for making models, for example. The clay keeps its new shape until it is squeezed or stretched again.

Bread dough is soft and easy to knead but changes when it is baked.

Hardening

When soft, wet dough is baked in an oven, the heat changes it. It becomes firm and turns into bread. The only way to change its shape now is by tearing or cutting it.

Soft, wet clay can be shaped into a pot. Once baked in a very hot oven, the pot cannot be squeezed or stretched again.

Elasticity

When some materials are stretched, their shape doesn't change forever. These materials have **elasticity**. When you stretch rubber and elastic, for example, they snap back to their original shape when you let go.

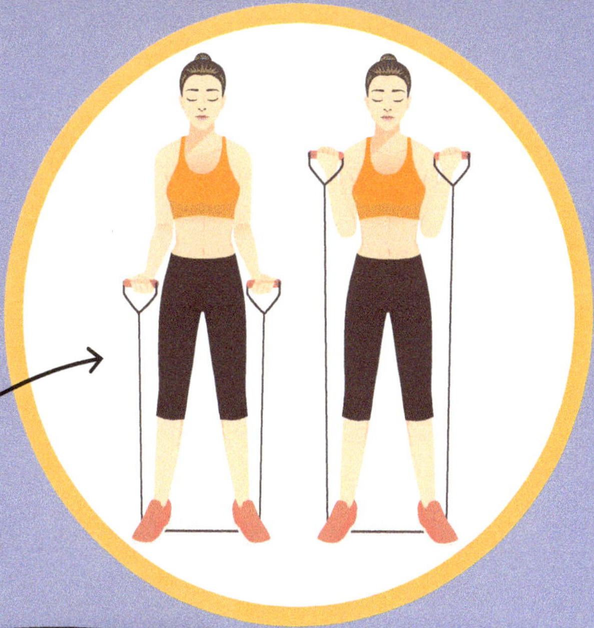

Once stretched, this elastic band goes back to its original size.

ACTIVITY

MAKE BOUNCING CREATURES

Ask an adult to help you with this activity.

You will need:

- **colored card stock**
- **colored pens or pencils**
- **scissors**
- **darning needle**
- **about 2.5 feet (0.75 m) of sewing elastic**
- **beads (for weight)**

1. Copy one of the animal shapes shown below onto the colored card stock. Cut it out and decorate it.

2. Ask an adult to use the darning needle to pierce a hole through the middle of the body.

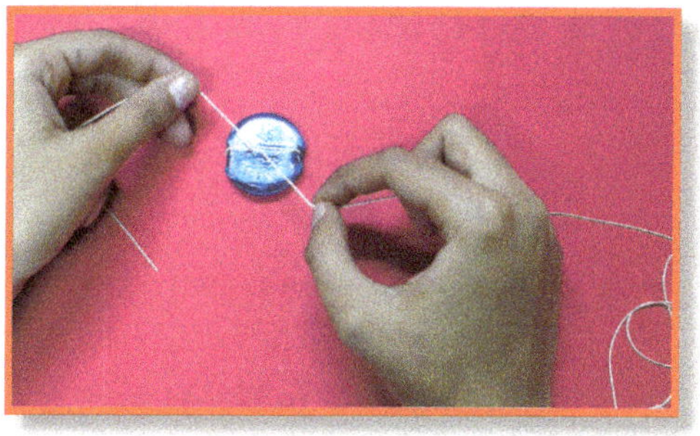

3. Tie one end of the sewing elastic to a big bead. Ask an adult to help you thread the other end through the hole, using a darning needle, from the underside of the body.

4. Bounce your creature up and down on the sewing elastic.

RECYCLING MATERIALS

We often use things and throw them away when we have finished with them. Instead of wasting the materials they are made of, it makes sense to use them to make something else.

Biodegradable plastic bags rot alongside this food waste.

Saving resources

Recycling means to break something down and use the materials to make something new. Many materials, such as paper, plastic, glass and metal, can be recycled. Recycling helps to save **resources**.

Natural materials

Biodegradable materials, such as paper and cotton, break down naturally and become part of the soil, water, or air. Some plastics are now made to be biodegradable.

Materials that can be recycled are collected regularly from households and taken to a recycling plant.

ACTIVITY

MAKE AND RECYCLE PAPER

Ask an adult to help you with this activity.

You will need:

- **used paper**
- **bowl of warm water**
- **egg beater**
- **rectangle of fine mesh (from your local hardware store or garden center)**
- **tray**
- **2 large sheets of blotting paper**
- **electric iron**

1. Tear the paper into small pieces and put them in a bowl of warm water. Leave to soak for a few minutes.

2. Ask an adult to help you beat the mixture with an egg beater to make a pulp.

3. Put the mesh into the tray. Pour the pulp onto the mesh and smooth it into a thin layer. Leave to drain.

4. Turn the mesh onto a sheet of blotting paper. Cover it with the other sheet of blotting paper. Ask an adult to help you press it with a warm iron.

5. Lift off the top sheet of blotting paper. When it has dried out thoroughly, you can use your paper.

MODERN MATERIALS

People have always made things from the materials they find around them–from stone and wood to grass and soil. Now, many new materials have been created for special uses.

Race cars

The first race cars were made of heavy metal. This slowed them down. Today, race cars are made of a new material called **carbon fiber**. It is strong and light and good for racing at high speeds.

Kevlar®

Kevlar® is another very strong, light material. It is made from a type of plastic, called nylon and is used to make helmets and body armor. It is much lighter and quieter than the heavy metal armor worn by knights long ago!

Smart materials

New materials have been developed that can change and respond to conditions around them. Memory metal, for example, is a **smart material** that "remembers" the shape it has been given. Memory metal is a good material for glasses frames that might get bent or twisted.

ACTIVITY

COMPARE MODERN MATERIALS

You will need:

- **sheet of paper**
- **ruler**
- **pencil or pen**
- **reference books**
- **computer**

1. Draw a chart like the one below. Use books and the internet to find information about each modern material.

2. Write notes about what the materials are made from, their properties and what they are used for. Some uses have been added for you, but there are others too.

Which material would be most useful to you and why?

	Made from	Properties	Used for
Kevlar®	Nylon	Strong, light	Helmets, body armor 
Nomex®			Firefighter gear 
Titanium			Professional racing bike 
Metal foam			Cars 
Memory metal			Glasses frame 

Glossary

absorbent

Materials that are absorbent soak up or take in liquid. A sponge is made of absorbent material.

biodegradable

Biodegradable materials break down or decay naturally and become part of the soil, water, or air.

boil

Liquids boil when they are heated to a high temperature. At their boiling point, they start to bubble and turn into gas.

carbon dioxide

Carbon dioxide is a gas in the air. We breathe out carbon dioxide and plants take it in. When fuels are burned, they give off carbon dioxide.

carbon fiber

Carbon fiber is a strong, light thread used to make other materials, such as metal, stronger.

dissolve

When a solid dissolves in a liquid, it becomes absorbed and makes a solution.

elasticity

Materials with elasticity can be stretched, pulled, or squeezed and will snap back to their original shape or size.

evaporate

A liquid evaporates when it is heated and changes into water vapor.

expand

When a material expands, it spreads out and becomes larger.

freeze

When liquids reach a low enough temperature, they freeze and become solid. This temperature is called the freezing point.

limestone

Limestone is a type of rock.

melt

When some solids are heated, they melt and become liquid. The temperature is called the melting point.

minerals

Minerals are solid substances, such as salt and tin, that are found naturally in rocks and in the ground.

mixture

A mixture contains different substances mixed together. You mix ingredients to make cake mixture, for example.

molten

Solids become molten when they are heated and melt into a liquid.

molded

Solids are molded by being melted, poured into a mold, and then left to cool and harden into the shape of the mold.

polystyrene foam

Polystyrene foam is a type of light plastic filled with bubbles of air.

properties

A material's properties describe what it is like.

resources

Resources are supplies of the things we use, such as metal, oil, or coal.

smart materials

Smart materials are made to sense what is going on around them and to change if necessary.

solution

A solution is made when a substance mixes with a liquid and dissolves completely.

stalactite

A stalactite is an icicle-shaped pillar hanging down from the roof of a cave, formed when minerals in dripping water are left behind.

stalagmite

Stalagmites are formed in the same way as stalactites. They grow up from the cave floor.

water vapor

Water vapor is water in the form of a gas. It is produced when water is heated.

waterproof

Waterproof materials do not absorb or soak up water.

Quiz

1. **Which are the three forms of materials?**

   a) solid
   b) space
   c) liquid
   d) gas

2. **Which is true?**

   a) liquids have a shape of their own
   b) liquids flow at the same speed
   c) water is only found as a liquid
   d) water freezes at 32°F (0°C)

3. **When air heats up it:**

   a) contracts
   b) expands
   c) sinks
   d) becomes heavier

4. **Glass is made from:**

   a) sand and limestone
   b) sand and water
   c) sand and oil
   d) sand and wood

5. **Which method of cooking is reversible?**

   a) heating soup
   b) baking a cake
   c) toasting bread
   d) boiling vegetables

6. **Dissolve means to:**

   a) fall apart
   b) disappear
   c) become wet
   d) mix completely

7. **Which material DOESN'T melt when heated?**

   a) glass
   b) plastic
   c) wood
   d) metal

8. **Recycling means to:**

   a) use less of something
   b) use more of something
   c) use something again
   d) use materials to make something new

9 **Biodegradable materials:**

a) break down naturally
b) don't break down naturally
c) are of high quality
d) are of low quality

10 **What would make a good race car?**

a) a strong, heavy material
b) a strong, light material
c) a strong, bendy material
d) a light, bendy material

ANSWERS | a/c/d, 2d, 3b, 4a, 5a, 6d, 7c, 8d, 9a, 10b

FURTHER INFORMATION

BOOKS

Be a Scientist: Investigating Materials by Jacqui Bailey, Wayland

Boom Science: Materials by Georgia Amson-Bradshaw, Franklin Watts

Extreme Science: Awesome Matter and Materials by Jon Richards, Wayland

Outdoor Science: Materials by Izzi Howell, Wayland

WEBSITES

All about materials: www.bbc.co.uk/bitesize/topics/zryycdm

Different materials and where they come from: www.lovemyscience.com/facts-materials.html

Find out more and test yourself: www.dkfindout.com/uk/science/materials

Index